My Guide Inside

Knowing Myself and Understanding My World
(Book II)
Intermediate Learner Book

Christa Campsall
and
Jane Tucker

3 Principles Ed Talks
myguideinside.com

CCB Publishing
British Columbia, Canada

My Guide Inside (Book II) Intermediate Learner Book

Copyright © 2016, 2020, 2024 by Christa Campsall – http://www.myguideinside.com
My Guide Inside® is a registered trademark of Christa Campsall (3 Principles Ed Talks)
ISBN-13   978-1-77143-589-5
Second Edition

Library and Archives Canada Cataloguing in Publication
Title: My guide inside (book II) intermediate learner book / by Christa Campsall and Jane Tucker.
Names: Campsall, Christa, author.
Issued in print and electronic formats.
ISBN 9781771435895 (softcover) | ISBN 9781771435901 (PDF)
Additional cataloguing data available from Library and Archives Canada

Authored with: Jane Tucker
Graphic Design: Josephine Aucoin
Production: Tom Tucker
Webmaster: Michael Campsall

E-books, MGI Online, Video on Demand Classes, Video Clips, and Digital Media Tools:
See www.**myguideinside**.com for information on these resources.

The author has taken extreme care to ensure that all information in this book is accurate and current at the time of publication. Neither the author nor the publisher can be held responsible for any errors or omissions. Likewise, no liability is assumed for any damage caused by the use of the information from this publication.

All rights reserved. No part of this work may be reproduced in any form – graphically, electronically or mechanically – or processed, duplicated or distributed using electronic systems without the written permission of the author, except for reviewers who may quote brief passages. Any request for photocopying, recording, taping or storage in information systems for any part of this work should be made in writing to the author at: **myguideinside.com**

Why an Owl? Over the years as a classroom teacher, Christa was given various owl gifts. She loves them as symbols of the wisdom we all share. Starting in ancient times and throughout history, various cultures have seen the owl as linked with wisdom and guidance. The owl's big, round eyes symbolize seeing knowledge. Although it is sometimes linked to other ideas, it is because of this connection to wisdom, guidance, and seeing knowledge that the owl was chosen as the graphic symbol for *My Guide Inside (MGI)*. Christa and Jane hope this interpretation is also meaningful to you.

Publisher: CCB Publishing
              British Columbia, Canada
              www.ccbpublishing.com

My Guide Inside® (Learner Book II)

Table of Contents

What kids say about discovering their inner wisdom… ... iv

Recognition and Thanks ... iv

Chapter 1 Discovering My Guide Inside ... 1

Chapter 2 Knowing the Most Wonderful Gift Ever ... 9

Chapter 3 Sharing = Caring ... 17

Chapter 4 Riding the Wave ... 25

Chapter 5 The Best Ship Is Friendship ... 35

Chapter 6 What a Difference an Insight Makes! ... 45

Chapter 7 Wheels of Learning Keep on Turning ... 53

Chapter 8 You Are a Wonder ... 59

Chapter 9 Power Words Enriching Your Life ... 65

End Notes for My Guide Inside ... 68

Overview of My Guide Inside® Comprehensive Curriculum ... 69

About the Authors and What Teachers Say ... 71

What kids say about discovering their inner wisdom…

- "I couldn't figure out this problem. So I put it down and then it came to me. If you have a calm mind you can work it out. With a calm mind there is more room to think."

- "This class has helped me…to not let myself get mad and to [not] have another person have an effect on me to ruin my day."

- "Your common sense guides you. I know common sense breaks your negative thoughts. It helps you get on with things and makes it easier."

- "I learned that if you lighten thoughts you sometimes feel better. It helped me know to calm down when I get mad."

- "A benefit of optimism is you can do the things you want to do because you know you can."

- "Let it go; don't let it grow!"

- "Almost every single idea or fact I have learned in this class has [helped] me already and will help me."

See what kids and teens think by watching two videos at myguideinside.com
My Guide Inside Overview (5min) and *My Guide Inside* Secondary Students Outcomes (5min).

Recognition and Thanks

The authors of this book knew a kind Canadian man with a soft Scottish accent and a twinkle in his eye, named Sydney Banks. He discovered Three Principles: Mind (wisdom), Consciousness (awareness) and Thought (creative tool), that are true for all people, and that can help us all live happy, successful lives.

He taught us that inner wisdom and happiness are inside everyone. Mr. Banks had great hope. He knew we could share the "joys of living" with each other. He knew the world would be a "far, far better place" when people learned to see the inner wisdom in themselves and others. In this book, inner wisdom is usually called ***my guide inside***!

Come on along!
Let's discover your guide inside. You will have a nicer life!
1. Your guide inside is always available. See what happens when you notice it.
2. You will have your own words to name your guide inside. It is natural inner wisdom.
3. Everyone has a healthy core of natural inner wisdom.

My Guide Inside® (Learner Book II)

**You are invited on a learning journey
leading to your own inner wisdom.**

You will learn to listen to your guide inside
and listen to learn to help you decide.

Solve this puzzle!

Se
cret.hid
den.in.p
lain.sig
ht.
It.is. guide.in
side.Listen.to.y
our.gu
ide.and.know.
you.are.a.wonder.

Let's discover your guide inside.
It's not hidden but it's sure worth finding.

Can you think of a time you felt happy and secure?
Do you feel this way right now?
You can, you know!

Quiet the chitter chatter and hear the inner voice, your guide inside. For example, when you shake a snow globe you see the snow, but not the scene. When you stop shaking it, the snow settles and you can see the scene clearly. When you let your mind settle, you can see life clearly. When your mind is clear; it is quiet. "A quiet mind hears the inner voice." (1)

My guide inside is sometimes hidden in plain sight until you know the secret! The secret is that my guide inside is always there. 24-7-365.

My guide inside has many different names in many different places.
What name do you like?

What name does the group like the most?

My Guide Inside
Common Sense
Wisdom
Insight
Inside Knowing
Intuitive Mind
Inside Sun
Little Voice Inside
Inner Voice
Healthy Core
or… think of new words!

My Guide Inside® (Learner Book II)

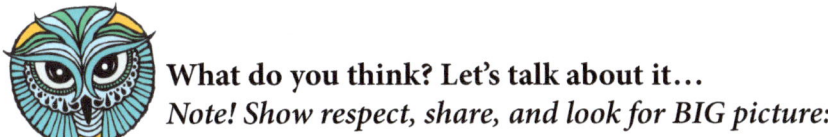

What do you think? Let's talk about it...
Note! Show respect, share, and look for BIG picture:

Your guide inside is powerful knowledge that grows with you.

Just as every apple has a core inside, every one of us has a healthy core inside…our common sense or inner wisdom. It is your guide inside. It is "powerful knowledge" that is helpful. Your wisdom "will grow with you and guide you to wonders beyond your imagination." (2)
Share ideas about what "guide inside" means.

Knowing about your guide inside, natural inner wisdom, can make your world a better place. It guides you to love and compassion … "two magical feelings that will help guide you through life." Love and compassion "may be caring for someone in need … Or it may be bringing a little joy to others …" (3)
What is a way to make your world a better place?

Wisdom also leads to the "joys of living."
Think of a time you were doing something that you enjoyed. Think of what you were doing, where you were, and who you were with. Think of how you were feeling.
Share with a partner.

When you are enjoying life, you feel happy.
Have you noticed that?

> We use thought to produce feelings! When you have a happy thought; you have a happy feeling. Try this out! It works every time. No guessing needed. It is a logical rule.

Sometimes, my guide inside seems clouded over.
I don't feel happy and secure, instead I feel unsure.
A cloudy thought causes a negative feeling:
"Nobody likes me," and I feel worry.
"I never understand," and I feel fear.
"This is always too hard," and I feel anger.

What is another cloudy thought?

Do you ever watch the white, fluffy clouds? They move, don't they?
At any time, you can let a thought pass by. This is like a cloud passing by in front of the sun. As soon as the cloudy thought passes by, "in its place comes a nicer thought that you act on." (4)

Practice is your friend!

When you first ride a bike, you may be a bit wobbly and it takes courage to try again. When you practice enough; you find your balance and …you never forget how!

When you first let a cloudy thought pass by, you may be a bit wobbly, and it takes courage to try again. When you trust inner wisdom; you find your balance and … you never forget how!

> "…if you can keep your mind clear of negative thoughts, such a state will fill your heart with the joys of living and guide you through life." (5)

Now You Know!

- Just as every apple has a core inside, every one of us has a healthy core of common sense and wisdom, called "my guide inside."
- Your guide inside is powerful knowledge, also known as wisdom.
  > It grows with you.
  > It brings you love and compassion.
  > It leads to the "joys of living."
- A cloudy thought passes by like clouds pass by the sun.
- "…if you can keep your mind clear of negative thoughts, such a state will fill your heart with the joys of living and guide you through life." (5)

Learn Power Words!

- ❂ aware—in the know, seeing what is
- ❂ compassion—caring
- ❂ common sense—knowing to make good choices, insight, my guide inside, wisdom
- ❂ feeling—sense
- ❂ guide—help
- ❂ insight—a helpful new idea, common sense, my guide inside, wisdom
- ❂ knowledge—intelligence, understanding
- ❂ logical—makes common sense
- ❂ my guide inside—common sense, insight, my wisdom
- ❂ secure—safe
- ❂ source—where something begins or comes from
- ❂ thought—power to create an idea
- ❂ wisdom—knowing what is true or right, common sense, insight, my guide inside

Resources Tab
myguideinside.com for Video On Demand and Digital Media Options. password: mgi

Reflect and Write a Journal Entry…
Note! Use "I." Share your thoughts and feelings. Show insight and connections.

Use two of the above Power Words in a journal entry about the BIG picture idea:
> ***My guide inside or wisdom is "powerful knowledge."***
> ***Wisdom "will grow with you and guide you."***

Activities

Write Your Thoughts…
Note! Show depth of thought, add details, and be clear.

Think of a time when you were doing something you enjoy. It can be something active, like playing a game, singing or dancing. Or it can be something quiet, like drawing, reading or being with your pet. Think about what you were doing. Think of where you were and who you were with. Think of how you were feeling.
Now write about it!

Create a Work of Art…
Note! Be original; show spirit; use the space; use color, shading or ink.

Think of a time you were feeling happy. It may be the time you just wrote about or a different time. It doesn't matter what you were doing, as long as you felt happy. Draw and color a picture of that happy time. Give the picture a title.

Create a Mural…
Note! Be clear, accurate and neat; use the space; make it colorful.

With a partner or a group, make an art mural to display. Use my guide inside or similar name for the center of the mural and decorate the border.

Have Fun!
Shake a snow globe! As you watch and the snow settles, you can see the scene clearly. Same is true for every one of us. When you let your mind settle; you can see life clearly.

Come on along!

Discover your gift of Thought. You will know what to choose!
1. You can drop an unhelpful thought like a hot potato and just act on the helpful ones.
2. It is natural to act on thoughts that bring happy and secure feelings.
3. You have used this common sense many times to make wise choices.

> Riddle Me This!
> This is a gift that each of us is born with.
> This is something we are using all the time, don't say "air!"
> We are using it when we are sleeping.
> We are using it when we are awake.
> We are using it when we are in school or at home.
> When we are alone, we are using it.
> What is it?

That's correct! Thought!

"Thought is a gift." (6)

Thought is the way every one of us knows ideas.

> Every one of us has the "gift of thought" to use as we choose.
> Imagine that!
> Humans can use thought to think up anything!
> My guide inside helps me decide.
> I choose which thought to use.

It is natural to act on thoughts that result in being happy and secure.

Thoughts create feelings. Give it a try.
Think a happy thought…it creates a happy feeling.
Think a fearful thought…it creates a fearful feeling.

Wesley's Story
Make pictures in your mind!

Devan has a little brother, Wesley, and he has a problem. There are monsters that live under his bed. At night when Wesley tries to go to sleep he can hear the monsters. They are under the bed just waiting to jump out and get him. The monsters scare him!

Every night, Wesley leaps from the light switch to the bed. He knows that he is safe as long as he keeps the blankets up to his neck. If an arm or leg slips out he is in big trouble. That is when the monsters can attack! Wesley feels fear at night. He stays awake wondering when the monsters are going to get him. Wesley is even starting to look sick because he is not sleeping.

Devan has compassion for his little brother and tries to help him. He tells him the monsters are make-believe. There are no monsters under his bed! He lifts up the blanket for him to look under it. This does not help. Wesley knows the monsters can become invisible so they can't be found. Devan also says, "Hey, Wes, you can drop a thought like a hot potato! You choose which thought to use."

Every night Wesley thinks about the monsters and he feels fear. Then one night, he remembers when he thought there was a dragon outside his window. He knew he saw it! When he jumped out of bed to close the window blinds, he saw it was not a dragon. It was the shadow of a cat and the branches of a tree. It only looked like a dragon. Maybe Devan was right. Maybe he was just using his own thoughts to scare himself.

Wesley laughed, and "POOF" the thought of a monster was gone! He even tried to bring it back to scare himself, but he couldn't. It was over! Devan came back in the room when he heard Wesley laughing. Wesley said he felt like he was being a scaredy cat! Devan laughed and said, "It's OK! We all feel like that sometimes! Like Dad says, "You've always got a chance to change your mind." Wesley was happy to hear that. Instead of feeling fear, he felt confident and he fell fast asleep. Z Z Z …

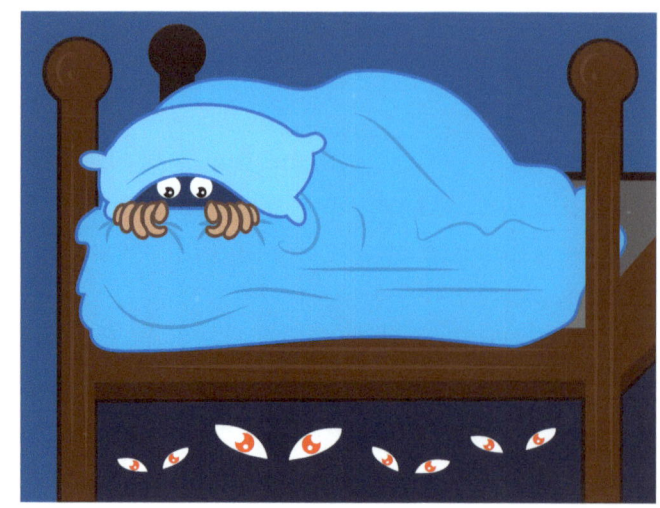

What do you think? Let's talk about it…

 *Note! Show respect, share, look for BIG picture:*

You have the gift of thought to use as you choose. Imagine that!

How is this story like something you know?
Finish these sentence starters and share with a partner:
I used to believe…
But, now I understand…

It's natural to outgrow ideas. Just like you used to believe some things were real and you now understand they were just your thoughts. It's common sense that it was make-believe. Sometimes a thought pops into your head that is not helpful. Don't be fooled by your own thinking.

Wesley's scary thoughts led to scary feelings.
He changed his mind, and then he felt the opposite; he felt confident!

> Let's have Opposite Day Today!
> Any day can be Opposite Day…
>
> Choose one and let's talk about it.
> You can feel positive, which is the opposite of feeling negative.
> You can feel at peace, instead of feeling angry.
> ~calm, not worried~
> ~confident, instead of fearful~
> ~happy, not unhappy~
> ~respect, instead of dislike~
> ~content, not uneasy~
> ~secure, instead of insecure~
> ~hopeful, not hopeless~
> Instead of feeling mean; you can feel kind.
> It is easy to have opposite day, if you just change your mind…

> Thought is a gift to use as you choose,
> Act on the good thoughts,
> And you'll have nothing to lose!

Wesley knows…

- Every one of us has the gift of thought to use as we choose. Imagine that!
- Thought is the way every one of us knows ideas.
- Thoughts create feelings.
- "You've always got a chance to change your mind."
- It's common sense to see which thoughts are make-believe.
- You can drop a thought like a hot potato!
- Act on the good thoughts.

…Now you know, too!

Learn Power Words!

- believe—accept as true
- common sense—knowing to make good choices, insight, wisdom
- confident—positive, sure of oneself
- content—satisfied and happy
- fooled—tricked
- imagination—creation in your mind
- negative—not helpful or useful
- positive—good or useful
- respect—see as worthy
- understand—to know

Resources Tab

myguideinside.com for Video On Demand and Digital Media Options. password: mgi

Reflect and Write a Journal Entry…

Note! Use "I." Share your thoughts and feelings. Show insight and connection.

Use two of the above Power Words in a journal entry about the BIG picture idea:
You have the gift of thought to use as you choose. Imagine that!

Activities

Write Your Thoughts…
Note! Show depth of thought, add details, and be clear.

Describe something that you remember making up.
Use the sentence starters:
I used to believe…
But, now I understand…

Create a Work of Art…
Note! Be original; show spirit; use the space; use color, shading or ink.

Fold the paper in half and draw "Opposite Day."
Show one half as negative and the other half positive.
For example: draw someone looking mean and draw someone looking kind.

Also, draw or color things as opposites in your pictures. For example: one picture: the moon, the other picture: the sun; one picture: a winter scene, the other a summer scene; one picture: a big person, the other a small person. Add your own ideas!

Have Fun!
Use play dough to make an animal. What ideas do you have for your animal? Are your ideas one of a kind compared to others in the group? Show that you can use the gift of thought to create any idea!

Chapter 3
Sharing = Caring

Come on along!

Notice a new insight. You will have a chance to feel calm and caring.
1. Your wisdom helps you choose to let a worrisome thought go.
2. Notice what happens when a better thought pops into your head.
3. When we listen to wisdom, caring and sharing happen naturally.

Tanis' Story
Listening with your whole self shows respect for the storyteller.

You, the listener, are the important keeper of the story.

Let's listen.

When Tanis was a little girl, she saw how happy her friends were when they had a chance to visit their grandmothers. One day, Tanis asked her mother if she could have her mother's aunty be her grandmother. Tanis didn't have a grandmother and she could feel the love from her mother's aunt.

Tanis' mother suggested she go ask Aunty if she would like that. Aunty lived nearby in the community. Tanis ran off to ask Aunty if she would like to be her Grandma. Tanis was happy when she said yes!

Each time Tanis saw Grandma, she was so happy to run to her and have a talk. She could talk to Grandma about anything and she always felt welcome.

Tanis told her mother, "Talking to an elder helps you know more. Grandma shares what she has learned about nature. Grandma sees how everything is connected—and I mean everything! She takes time to sit with me when I have worried or angry thoughts. She's teaching me that thought is a spiritual gift and that I can choose which thought to use. I don't have to act on all of them!"

"It is like a gift of understanding, Tanis!" said her mother. She could see how time with her Grandma was helping Tanis feel happy. She saw it in Tanis' smile and her sparkling eyes.

At school, Tanis felt happy creating a picture for Grandma. It was her 75th birthday on the weekend, and Tanis wanted to give her something special.

She painted Grandma sitting on the porch swing, looking up at the sky just as the sun was setting. Tanis had seen her sitting just like that many times.

Tanis was proud of her painting. It really did look like her grandmother, and the colors in the sky were so bright. Then, her classmate bumped into the cup holding the brushes and the water ruined her painting! Tanis was upset. It was the end of the school day and she went home feeling sad, and worried she wouldn't have a gift. Tanis' dad listened to her story of what happened. He said, "Why don't you go over to Grandma's and tell her about it? I am sure she will understand. You could bring her some flowers from the garden."

Tanis had to admit it was a good idea. She walked down the street with her little bunch of daisies and she saw Grandma sitting on her front porch, looking out at the late afternoon sky. Seeing Grandma on her porch swing usually made Tanis feel happy, but this time it just reminded her of her ruined picture, and she felt even worse.

Grandma smiled as Tanis came near. "Hi there," she said warmly. "What lovely flowers! Did you pick them for me?"

Tanis nodded and handed the daisies to her, without looking at her. "Thank you so much," Grandma said. "What's happening today?"

"I was going to give you a gift. I painted a beautiful picture of you looking up at the many sunset colors. Then water spilled on it and all the colors ran together. It's ruined!" Tanis answered, and she felt upset again as she said it.

Grandma patted the porch swing to invite Tanis to sit beside her. "How loving you are to make a picture of me. I will never forget such a special gift."

"But it's ruined!" Tanis repeated.

Grandma compassionately said, "You've told me about it, and I can see it in my mind. I know you can have a vision for another picture."

"What is a vision, Grandma?" asked Tanis.

"Well, you know how you thought about painting me and the sunset, and you had a feeling about it, and then a picture came to mind? That's what a vision is. It's a picture formed in your mind," said Grandma.

Tanis sat quietly listening to nature and looking at the birds circling high in the sky. The sun popped out from behind the clouds. Tanis had an insight that her good feelings were like the sun, sometimes they got clouded over with a thought of worry. Just like a cloud passes by, so will a thought of worry! She knew that there is always the chance to feel calm again.

She felt loved as she sat there with Grandma. She always came away from these visits with a better understanding.

Grandma gave Tanis a little hug. "I get so much from your visits, Dear One. I love it when you come see me."

Tanis' eyes sparkled. "I do too, Grandma. We're both giving and receiving and that makes it a circle, doesn't it?"

"That's right, Tanis, it is a circle," answered Grandma. She was happy her granddaughter was learning so much about life and knew it would help Tanis to understand her world.

Just then, Tanis had a vision for a new picture. She would paint Grandma and the people she loved in a circle, with the sun setting behind them. She jumped up, turned and hugged her Grandma, and kissed her cheek. "Got to go, Grandma! I just thought of something I want to do. Bye! Love you."

"Bye! Love you, too!"

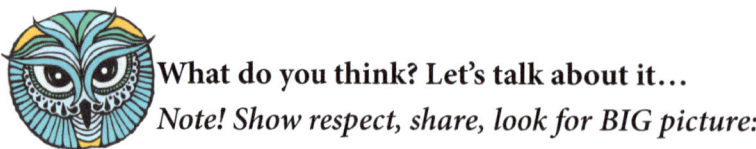 **What do you think? Let's talk about it…**
Note! Show respect, share, look for BIG picture:

Giving and receiving make a circle.

How is this story like something you know?
This story shows the value of sharing. What is shared in the story?

"Just like a cloud passes by, so will a thought of worry! She knew that there is always the chance to feel calm again." Think of a time you noticed this in your life.

 **Tanis knows…**
- You may have thoughts of worry sometimes. Other people can guide you inside to your calm feelings, like Tanis' Grandma helped her.
- You can help yourself, like Tanis did when she had the insight that her good feelings were like the sun.
- There is always a chance to feel calm again.
- Let go of old thoughts and be open to new ones.
- Insights are helpful for knowing ourselves and understanding our world.
- Giving and receiving make a circle.

…Now you know, too!

Learn Power Words!
- calm—quiet
- insight—wisdom, new understanding
- respect—honor
- spiritual—inner
- vision—idea
- worry—upset

Resources Tab
myguideinside.com for Video On Demand and Digital Media Options. password: mgi

Reflect and Write a Journal Entry…
Note! Use "I." Share your thoughts and feelings. Show insight and connections.

Use two of the above Power Words in a journal entry about the BIG picture idea:

Giving and receiving make a circle.

Activities

Tell a Story…
Note! Be willing; join in; have beginning, middle, and end; show confidence.

Retell the story with a partner. One person can tell the beginning and part of the middle, the other person can tell part of the middle and the end. Share the storytelling another way, if you choose. Listen to each other; hear new ideas.

Create Art for Sharing…
Note! Be original; show spirit; use the space; use color, shading or ink.

Make a picture, bookmark, sculpture, or other gift to share with someone in your family or community. How did you feel making the gift?

Have Fun!
Add a greeting card to the gift you made and have fun giving the surprise gift.

How did the person feel when receiving your gift?

Chapter 4
Riding the Wave

Come on along!

Thinking too much can cover up your guide inside. Feelings let us know!
1. You can be naturally aware of your feelings.
2. It is easy to notice when feelings are changing.
3. Learn to "*Huli the bowl!*" so helpful thoughts can create well-being.

Koa's Story*
What do you already know about the Hawaiian Islands?

Koa was born on the island of Maui, in Hawai'i. He took his first steps outside under the warm sun, on the soft grass in his family's backyard. He was a happy, laughing baby, always ready to explore and learn and climb around. He loved going to the beach with his family, playing on the sand and running into the foam of the waves as they crashed to shore. His young life was full of beautiful feelings and joy.

Koa had a brother, Kimo, who was a couple of years older. They played together all the time, and Koa really looked up to Kimo. Sometimes, when they were playing a game, Koa wouldn't understand the rules or would make mistakes. Kimo would become impatient, and tell his little brother, "No, you fool! That's not how you do it." This happened so many times that Koa came to believe he wasn't very smart. Playing games became less fun, because he worried about making mistakes. His beautiful feelings began to be overshadowed.

Koa started getting angry when he made mistakes, and his aunty told him, "You'd better watch that temper of yours." He heard her talking to his mom, saying, "Koa has a bad temper. I'm afraid it's going to get him in trouble." Koa believed what he heard, and now he carried around the thought that he had a bad temper, and would get in trouble because of it. Every time he got angry, he thought this was just the way it had to be, because of his bad temper. He thought his bad temper was a fact, not just a thought, and even though he tried to control it, he often felt he couldn't.

At school, the thought, "I'm not so smart," got in the way of Koa's learning. Like clouds blocking the sun, it covered up his inner intelligence. He worried so much about making mistakes that he didn't hear what the teacher was saying. When he tried to read, his mind was too busy to focus on the letters and the words.

Koa often got angry with his classmates, acting as if he had a bad temper, because that's what he thought was true. He didn't have many friends because he was angry so much. He also got angry at himself, because he couldn't seem to control his temper, and because he wasn't getting good grades.

By now, Koa's beautiful feelings of joy were covered over most of the time. The only time he felt happy and free was at the beach, when he would swim in the ocean and ride the waves into shore. His uncle had shown him how to surf, teaching him about clearing his mind of any fearful thoughts, and becoming "one" with the wave. This was the only way to stay up on a surfboard. Of course, everybody falls down sometimes, and Koa's uncle made sure his nephew understood this. "No shame wiping out!" he laughed. "Everybody falls down. You just get up again and catch the next wave. Forget about the last one!"

One Saturday, after a wonderful afternoon surfing with his uncle, Koa said, "I wish we could just live at the beach and surf all day, every day. I hate school. I'm too stupid to learn anything and I have a horrible temper."

"What!" His uncle's eyes opened wide. "You—stupid? No way. You are one smart surfer. You watch the waves, and know which ones to catch, which ones to let pass. You couldn't surf like that if you weren't smart. And 'horrible temper?' Who told you that? I never see you get mad, even when you wipe out and get all tumbled around in the waves."

Koa couldn't believe his ears. Did his uncle really think he was smart? And thinking about it, Koa realized that he never did get mad when he was out surfing. He just enjoyed what he was doing, and didn't care if he fell down or made mistakes.

"But Uncle, school is so different from surfing," Koa said sadly. "I'm not smart in school."

"Nonsense!" said his uncle. "The same intelligence that helps you surf can help you with your schoolwork. It's right inside of you, all the time."

"Well, it sure doesn't feel like it. I get so mad at school, 'cause I never have the right answers. Everybody thinks I'm stupid."

"Thoughts like that are what keep you from learning!" said his uncle, reaching over and tousling Koa's hair. "Let me tell you a story. It's something my grandma told me when I was just a little boy. She heard it from her own grandparents when she was small. It's about something strong and powerful inside every new baby that comes into the world. This is how my grandma explained it:

"Every child is born with a bowl of light inside of him or her. That bowl of light can never go away. It is full of *Aloha* (Love) and wisdom and beauty. When it shines, you feel good, and you know what to do. As children grow older, they start to think too much about themselves. They might start to think they are not as good as others, or that they aren't smart, or that they are too short, or too tall, or that nobody likes them. Now, everybody has a thought like that once in a while, and if you're wise, you just let that kind of thought pass—like when you know a wave isn't good for surfing, so you let it go by and wait for a good one. Know what I mean?"

Koa nodded his head.

"Good. Well, if you don't let go of those negative thoughts, but hang onto them instead, it's like putting big, gray rocks inside your bowl of light. If you put enough rocks into the bowl, what do you think will happen to the light?"

Koa was quiet for a minute; then he said, "It will get all covered up."

"Exactly!" smiled his uncle. "Now, if you want to see that light shining again, what should you do? Should you take each rock, turn it around and around in your hands, look at it, try to remember where you got it…or should you just *huli* (turn over) the bowl?" He made a motion with his hands, as if he were turning a bowl upside down and dumping everything out.

"*Huli* the bowl!" shouted Koa.

"Yes, my boy. *Huli* the bowl. Forget about all those beliefs that make you feel less than you are, and let your light shine."

His uncle's words, so full of warmth and *aloha*, helped Koa feel much better. He could feel the "bowl of light" inside him growing brighter, and he smiled. It gave him hope that things could change.

On Monday, as he walked into his classroom, Koa started to feel the same old bad feelings. He was thinking about how hard the work would be, and that he would get all the wrong answers again. This time, though, he remembered what his uncle had said about letting a wave pass if it wasn't a good one. He knew that right that minute he had a chance to change, and he found the courage to take that chance. Instead of thinking about how hard the work would be, he let his mind quiet down, and remembered the bowl of light, inside. The moment he did that, he was filled with a wonderful feeling. All of a sudden, he knew he could learn.

That morning was the best morning Koa had ever had at school. His mind was quiet enough that he could hear what the teacher was saying, and he even raised his hand to answer questions. When he had trouble with a math problem, instead of getting mad or giving up, he raised his hand again, and waited patiently until the teacher could get to him. As she asked him guiding questions, he discovered how to solve the problem!

At recess, Koa joined a kickball game with some classmates, and when he got "out," he didn't get angry at all. He felt so full of *aloha* and kindness that he didn't want to hurt anyone's feelings. His classmates were surprised at how nice he was being, and they became nicer to him.

The rest of the day went just as well. Koa had found something very valuable that would help him the rest of his life. From then on, he understood that no matter what anyone said, and no matter what mistaken thoughts might pop into his head, there was a spiritual light within him full of love, intelligence, and beauty.

Whenever he got in a low mood, or got discouraged, or got angry, he knew it was only his thoughts creating the feelings, and that deep down inside, he had a better answer. When he was ready, he could *huli* the bowl, dump out those gray rocks, and let his light shine.

---

*The "Bowl of Perfect Light" is a very old Hawaiian teaching that has been passed down from "kupuna" (grandparents or elders) to children for generations, to help them live a happy life. It is written about in a book called *Tales from the Night Rainbow* by Koko Willis and Pali Jae Lee, pages 18-19.

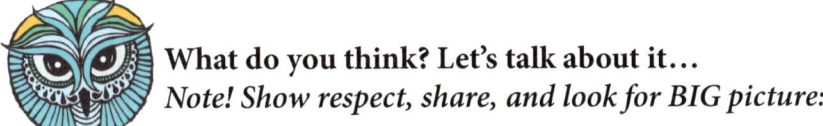

What do you think? Let's talk about it…
Note! Show respect, share, and look for BIG picture:

Every child is born with a "bowl of light" filled with aloha and wisdom.

How is this story like something you know?

Describe having an angry or worried thought and letting it pass by.

"I'm stupid." "Nobody likes me." "I can't understand."
Have you ever heard someone say something like that? What choice does the person have?

How can you get your "bowl of light" to shine again?

Koa knows…
- Every child is born with a "bowl of light" full of *aloha* and wisdom.
- When you have a thought of fear, worry, or anger; you can show courage.
- You can let your mind clear by letting a thought pass like a wave.
- Notice that you are able to "*Huli* the bowl!"
- This leads to actions you will be happy with…success!

…Now you know, too!

Learn Power Words!
- *aloha*—love (*Aloha* is a Hawaiian word)
- courage—power
- *huli*—turn around, turn over (*Huli* is a Hawaiian word)
- joy—happiness
- overshadowed—covered up
- patient—calm
- temper—state of mind (angry or calm)

Resources Tab
myguideinside.com for Video On Demand and Digital Media Options. password: mgi

Reflect and Write a Journal Entry…
Note! Use "I." Share your thoughts and feelings. Show insight and connections.

Use two of the above Power Words in a journal entry about the BIG picture idea:

Every child is born with a "bowl of light" filled with aloha and wisdom.

Activities

Write Your Thoughts…
Note! Show depth of thought, add details, and be clear.

With a partner, write a new story of someone learning about the "bowl of light." Decide who will learn about the "bowl of light" in your story. Make the story your own. Create the setting as here and now, in your world, and change story ideas.

Retell the Story…
Note! Be willing; join in; have logical beginning, middle, and end; show confidence.

Practice retelling the story with your partner. One person can tell the beginning and part of the middle, the other person can tell part of the middle and the end. Or, divide the retelling of the story another way, you choose. Share with an audience.

Create a Work of Art…
Note! Be original; show spirit; use the space; use color, shading or ink.

Draw and color your own "bowl of light."

More Art to create…
Note! Be original; show spirit; be unique, show design in the form.

Shape your own "bowl of light" out of clay. Don't forget the "rocks!"

Have Fun!
Look through a kaleidoscope. Turn the kaleidoscope and notice how it changes what you see. The same is true for us. When you feel serious, the world looks serious. Turn the kaleidoscope. When you have worried thoughts, the world feels and looks unsafe. Turn the kaleidoscope again. When you feel happy, the world looks like a beautiful place. Every one of us has our own world that we see with our own eyes!

Where do your feelings come from? From the kaleidoscope of your own thoughts. When you notice a new thought the feeling changes. That is how insights—helpful thoughts out of the blue that just pop into our heads from our inner wisdom—can help us out!

My Guide Inside® (Learner Book II)

Come on along!

Knowing when to "Stop, Wait, Go" makes a big difference.
1. Friends use their guide inside to make choices together.
2. Friends acting from calm thinking show understanding and kindness.

Signal Story
Make pictures in your mind!

Darius was sitting in class reading, when a pencil rolled off his desk onto the floor. Jerry, who sat beside him, picked up the pencil and put it on his own desk. Darius whispered to Jerry, "That's mine! Give it back."

Jerry just laughed and whispered, "Finders keepers."

"Give it back, now!" Darius whispered louder. His face was getting hot and he was starting to feel angry.

Still grinning, Jerry replied, "Make me!"

Darius reached over and grabbed for the pencil, but Jerry snatched it up and held it in the air, out of reach. Darius got half-out of his seat and grabbed Jerry's arm, and this is when their classmate noticed the ruckus.

"Hey, let go of his arm," said their classmate.

"He took my pencil!" Darius exclaimed, but he let go of Jerry's arm.

"Did not!" said Jerry. "I found it on the floor." He put the pencil back on Darius's desk. "Here—you can have it, you baby."

This made Darius feel even angrier. He felt that Jerry should get in trouble. He gave Jerry an angry look, and decided he would get back at him, somehow.

Signal Story: Replay
Predict how part two will be different.

Darius was sitting in class reading, when a pencil rolled off his desk onto the floor. Jerry, who sat beside him, picked up the pencil and put it on his own desk. Darius whispered to Jerry, "That's mine! Give it back."

Jerry just laughed and whispered, "Finders keepers."

Darius started to feel his face getting hot and he was starting to feel angry. He remembered something he was learning at school—that angry feelings are a signal to STOP and let your mind clear. He turned away from Jerry, looked out the window at the rain falling on the grass and trees outside, and he felt calm again. He forgot about the pencil for now—he wasn't using it anyway—and went back to his reading.

Jerry actually liked Darius and wanted to be friends with him. He thought if he fooled around and pretended to steal Darius's pencil, Darius would think he was funny. When Darius ignored him and just looked out the window, Jerry realized he had made a mistake, and put the pencil back on Darius's desk.

Darius was feeling at peace by this time, and he smiled at Jerry when he returned the pencil. He understood, now, that Jerry wasn't really going to keep it. Maybe it was just the only way he could think of to try and be friendly. Darius decided to ask Jerry if he wanted to come over after school.

My Guide Inside® (Learner Book II)

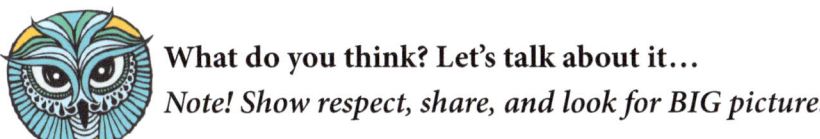

What do you think? Let's talk about it…
Note! Show respect, share, and look for BIG picture.

You can make a healthy decision and make a healthy friendship.

How is this story like something you know?

In the replay of the *Signal Story*, what did Darius remember that made everything different?

When you start to feel angry, stop, and let your mind clear. Inner wisdom shows the choice you have to solve the problem peacefully.

> RED light signal …STOP when angry!
> YELLOW light signal…What might this mean?
> GREEN light signal…GO ahead when at peace!

Think of a time it would be helpful to remember the signals.
You can change your mind and decide how to go ahead. You choose which thought to use.
It's common sense to act on the good thoughts!

Reflect and Write a Journal Entry…
Note! Use "I." Share your thoughts and feelings. Show insight and connections.

Write two good ideas about beginning a friendship.

Changing Your Mind Story
Connect what is read with what you already know!

Emily and Sofia are best friends. They sit together at lunch and play together on the playground. One day at school, a new girl named Cora comes into class. Emily sees Sofia smiling at Cora and being friendly to her.

Emily starts to worry that if Sofia and Cora become friends, she will be left out. She remembers being left out by friends when she was younger, and she's afraid it will happen again.

Emily is busy thinking and feels insecure. When she is called on to read, she doesn't know where to begin because she has only been thinking about her worries. Her thoughts become even more upset.

At lunch time, she and Sofia are sitting together, and Cora walks toward them. Emily says to Sofia, "Don't let her sit with us. She'll just try to butt in and spoil our fun." She puts her sweater down on the empty chair and tells Cora, "You can't sit here. It's saved."

Cora looks sad and walks away. Emily laughs and says to Sofia, "Don't you think she's kind of a baby?" Sofia feels compassion for the new girl. She's surprised that Emily is being so mean, because Emily is usually nice and fun to be around. Then she remembers, at school she is learning that when people act in hurtful ways, it's because their thinking is confused.

Sofia understands that maybe Emily is thinking fearful thoughts and feeling unsure. She says, "You and I are so lucky to be friends. That new girl is probably sad because she doesn't know anyone yet. We could share a feeling of belonging with her."

Emily feels better when Sofia acts so kind to her. She starts to see how Cora must be feeling. At this point, Emily has a choice. She can hold onto the bad memory of being left out when she was younger, or let it go. She has the courage to choose wisely, and calls out to the new girl, "Hey, Cora! The seat is actually not saved. Come sit with us!"

By the way…this was the start of a great friendship for these three girls!

What do you think? Let's talk about it…

Note! Show respect, share, and look for BIG picture:

We can make healthy decisions and make and keep healthy friendships

How is this story like something you know?"
It would help Emily to know: "Always cast away bad memories that dwell in your heart from your past… if you can keep your mind clear of negative thoughts, such a state will fill your heart with the joys of living…" (7)
Talk about a way this can also help you.

These kids know…

- RED light … STOP when angry!
- YELLOW light …What might this mean?
- GREEN light … GO ahead when at peace!
- It is easy to begin healthy friendships when you are welcoming.
- Keeping a healthy friendship is easy when you are friendly and kind.

…Now you know, too!

Learn Power Words!
- belonging—be a part of
- healthy—good
- insecure—unsure
- realize—see, understand
- signal—sign

Resources Tab
myguideinside.com for Video On Demand and Digital Media Options. password: mgi

Reflect and Write a Journal Entry…
Note! Use "I." Share your thoughts and feelings. Show insight and connections.

Use two of the above Power Words in a journal entry about the BIG picture idea:

We can make healthy decisions and make and keep healthy friendships.

Activities

Share…
Note! Be willing, tell ideas clearly, have confidence.

What makes a healthy friendship? How can you keep a healthy friendship?

Create a Poster…
Note! Share information, be colorful, use the space, be accurate.

Make a poster for younger kids on beginning and keeping healthy friendships. Include the title "The Best Ship is Friendship" and two or three good ideas.

Have Fun!
Learn an active game that can be played by every one in the group at a break. Play the game together and have fun!

Chapter 6
What a Difference an Insight Makes!

Come on along!

Know who and what you are. You have well-being inside.
1. Trust you do have personal well-being inside.
2. You can accept support and make a healthy choice at any time!
3. You will experience well-being by taking notice of your own insights.

Jake's Story
Reflect on the change in Jake!

Jake's dad gave him a skateboard for his birthday. He gained know-how and got the hang of it quickly! There was a skateboard park next to the school. Every day at recess, lunch and after school, Jake would put on his helmet, knee and elbow pads and wrist guards, and skate at the park.

Even the older kids were amazed at how well Jake rode. He would glide up the curved ramp, spin around in the air at the top, and shoot down again, making it look so easy! He loved the feeling of moving so fast, and when his board spun in the air, he felt like he was flying! Skateboarding was Jake's favorite thing to do. Sometimes there were contests at the park, and Jake came in first every time for his age group. Some of Jake's friends from school also skateboarded, and they asked him to teach them tricks. He was happy to show them. "Kids really like me because I'm so good at this," he thought.

One day there was a new boy in Jake's class named Carlos, and he came to the park. Carlos was smaller than Jake. He had a brightly colored board. Jake smiled and waved to him, and he waved back. Soon they were both riding on the ramps. Jake was surprised to see that Carlos could do so many tricks. He even did lots of new things that Jake had never seen before. The other kids in the park stopped skating to watch Carlos, and Jake did, too.

Then, a strange thing happened. Jake started to feel shaky and sick in his stomach, and he didn't feel like skateboarding anymore. He picked up his board and slowly walked out of the park, toward home.

Jake's grandfather was working in the kitchen when he looked through the window and saw Jake coming. "Home already?" he asked, as Jake came in the door.

Jake mumbled an answer and went into the living room.

His grandfather followed him. He sat down beside Jake on the sofa, and watched a show with him for a while. At a break, he turned to Jake, asking,

My Guide Inside® (Learner Book II)

"So, how was the park?" Jake was silent for a minute, then he turned to his grandfather and said, "Grandpa, there's a new kid in school who came to the park. He's in my class, so he's my age or maybe even younger, and he skates better than me!" As he spoke, he felt upset, and he quickly looked away.

"Oh, so that's it!" Grandpa laughed gently. "We all can feel a little shaky at times," he said. "But just because someone can skateboard a little better, that doesn't take anything away from you!"

"You don't understand!" Jake shouted. "He'll win all the contests now, and nobody will think I'm special anymore. I won't have any friends!"

"Jake, there's more to being a friend than being great at something and winning contests! Your friends like you because you are welcoming, you help them skate, and you're fun, too! Who and what you really are inside is what counts," said Grandpa compassionately.

Jake turned away from Grandpa and stared at the show. All he could think about was how good the new boy was on the ramps, and how every one had stopped to watch him. Jake decided he would never go back to the park again.

The next day was Saturday. Jake woke up and was thinking that it would be a good day for skateboarding. Then, his heart sank as he remembered—he had decided never to skate again. Jake looked at the sun shining through his window. Then another thought popped into his head. "Just because someone else can skateboard better, that doesn't take anything away from you! Who and what you really are inside is what counts."

Now, Jake felt those insightful words were true. He felt much better! Jake jumped out of bed, threw the comforter over it and went down to have some breakfast.

"Good morning, Jake!" said Grandpa, who was already sitting at the table, eating oatmeal. "Going somewhere?"

"Skateboarding!" answered Jake. "Soon as I'm done eating." Grandpa smiled. Just then there was a knock at the door.

"I'll get that," said Grandpa.

He opened the door to see Jake's friend, Tyrone, and the new boy, Carlos, standing with their skateboards. "Can Jake come out?"

"I'll be there in a minute!" Jake called to them. He finished breakfast, grabbed his board and safety gear, and headed out the door. "See you later, Grandpa... and thanks!"

"You're welcome, boy!" chuckled Grandpa. "Have fun!"

 **What do you think? Let's talk about it...**
Note! Show respect, share, and look for BIG picture:
   Who and what you are inside is what counts.

How is this story like something you know?

What a difference a day makes! Sometimes a good night's sleep changes how you see things. When you let your mind clear, an insight helps you make good choices.

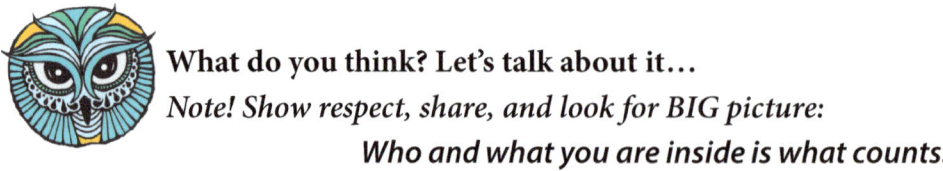 **Jake knows...**
Who and what you are inside is what counts!
   Anyone can gain know-how without it taking anything away from us.
   An insight helps us make good choices.

   ...Now you know, too!

Learn Power Words!
- compassionately—with caring
- insightful—wise
- "know-how"—knowledge or skill
- upset—worried

Resources Tab
myguideinside.com for Video On Demand and Digital Media Options. password: mgi

Reflect and Write a Journal Entry...
Note! Use "I." Share your thoughts and feelings. Show insight and connections.
Use one of the above Power Words in a journal entry about the BIG picture idea:

   Who and what you are inside is what counts.

Activities

Write Your Thoughts…
Note! Show depth of thought, add details, and be clear.

Read about an activity or skill you would like to learn. Perhaps it is an activity or skill that you are learning now. Write about what is needed to learn this and really gain know-how. What makes learning fun for you?

Create a Work of Art…
Note! Be original; show spirit; use the space; use color, shading or ink.

Look at pictures about the activity or skill you wrote about above. Create a picture about it and give the picture a title.

Have Fun!
Learn how to do the cat's cradle string game purrfectly. Learn it well and teach someone how to play. Or … learn and teach a new game of your choice!

You know who you are inside is what counts; then, it is easy to have fun while learning and gaining know-how!

Come on along!

Learn to recognize your state of mind. Know it by the feeling you are in.
1. When you focus attention, you will be aware of changes in your feelings.
2. This means you are naturally listening to your guide inside.
3. Helpful insights improve your feelings and natural motivation.

Amara's Story
Predict what will be learned!

Once there was a girl named Amara who loved life. She saw her world as a playground just waiting to be discovered. In the summer, she liked to sing and play all day. She would look up at the clouds and imagine things. She had fun looking for patterns in nature as she played.

Amara loved that there was so much to learn, and she even learned to solve hard problems. Her wheels of learning were really turning! Life was easy for her! She felt joy in her life when she was learning with her friends, and also when she was learning on her own.

Amara knew people who wanted to teach her about life. They all had very different ideas. Her cousin was serious and he thought that was the only way to be. He told Amara that she needed to "buckle down" and be serious with her work. Amara's sister was often worried about "running out of time." Hearing her sister worry, Amara started to think that was the way to be.

Her brother said, "Think about yourself. Put yourself first!"

Her friends said, "Think like this! Act like that!"

As Amara started to believe what everyone was telling her, she did become serious. She did start to worry. She did start to think only about herself. She found herself thinking, thinking, thinking. She felt the wheels of learning slow down. She started to worry, "Am I doing this right?" She felt unhappy.

One day Amara was outside with her Mom, playing with her baby brother who was in the kiddie pool. Amara would hold the rubber ducky under the water and then let it go. The baby started to giggle as the rubber ducky kept popping up in the water.

Suddenly, Amara was filled with happy feelings once again. With the return of these feelings, Amara had an insight: happy feelings can pop up anytime.

She said, "Mom, I just realized I can be happy. Just like the rubber ducky keeps popping up, my happiness keeps popping up!"

Amara looked into her Mom's kind eyes as she said, "Yes, nice feelings are inside every one of us. When you make good use of your own common sense, you do feel good. When you listen to other people so much, you can get confused. Then, it is best to let the mind clear." Her mom sang a little tune, "my guide inside is helping me decide! Sooooo…Only if it's useful will I keep that thought alive!" and danced in a circle. Now both the baby and Amara were giggling!

Amara let her mind clear and was just quiet. She glanced at the clouds, and then at her laughing little brother. She had happy feelings once again. She was excited that her wheels of learning keep on turning!

Amara was grateful toward life. She understood that she could trust her common sense. Amara whistled a happy tune and then sang out, "my guide inside is helping me decide! Sooooo…Only if it's useful will I keep that thought alive!"

What do you think? Let's talk about it...
Note! Show respect, share, and look for BIG picture:

"Sometimes it was only their thoughts that were making them unhappy and if they could understand...it would help make them feel well." (8)

How is this story like something you know?

Think of a time that you noticed your wheels of learning really turning.

Amara knows...
- Sometimes it is only your thoughts that make you unhappy.
- "My guide inside helps me decide!"
- It is best to let the mind clear when you are confused.
- Happiness is inside every one of us and keeps popping up.
- Trust common sense.
- Learning is easier when you feel joy in life.

...Now you know, too!

Learn Power Words!
- confused—not clear
- decision—a choice
- grateful—feeling thanks
- ignore—do nothing
- serious—stern
- welcoming—kind

Resources Tab
myguideinside.com for Video On Demand and Digital Media Options. password: mgi

Reflect and Write a Journal Entry...
Note! Use "I." Share your thoughts and feelings. Show insight and connections.

Use two of the above Power Words in a journal entry about the BIG picture idea:

"Sometimes it was only their thoughts that were making them unhappy and if they could understand...it would help make them feel well." (8)

Activities

Write a Poem...
Note! Show depth of thought, be organized, use colorful language, create a mood.

Write a poem about "Thought." Example Ideas:

- Thought is like a seed...
- Thought is a gift...
- A thought alone has no life of its own...
- You choose which thought to use...
- Act on the good thoughts...

Publish your poem and decorate the border. Display it for others to enjoy.

Recite a Poem...
Note! Be prepared, be accurate, speak clearly, be confident.

Memorize your poem and recite it to a group.

Create a Work of Art...
Note! Be original; show spirit; use the space.

Create a picture to illustrate the poem you wrote. Give the picture the same title as the poem.

Have Fun!
Blow up an an eco-friendly balloon, do not tie it, then let the air out! The air squeaks, hisses and fizzles out. How is this like your thinking?

When you take your focus away, the thought just fizzles out. A thought alone has no life of its own!

Chapter 8
You Are a Wonder

Come on along!

Look at you! See how much you have discovered about you!
1. Your guide inside is always present.
2. Thought is a gift and we have the choice of which thoughts to act on.
3. Insights help us know ourselves and understand our world.
4. Understanding thought and using insights makes life fun.
5. Your guide inside helps you be confident and optimistic about learning and friendship.
6. You know it is worthwhile to listen to your own common sense!

Chapters 1-7 Handy Reminders

Chapter 1: Let's discover your guide inside. You will have a nicer life!
    Your guide inside is always available. See what happens when you notice it.
    You will have your own words to name your guide inside. It is natural inner wisdom.
    Everyone has a healthy core of natural inner wisdom.

Chapter 2: Discover your gift of Thought. You will know what to choose!
    You can drop an unhelpful thought like a hot potato and just act on the helpful ones.
    It is natural to act on thoughts that bring happy and secure feelings.
    You have used this common sense many times to make wise choices.

Chapter 3: Notice a new insight. You will have a chance to feel calm and caring.
    Your wisdom helps you choose to let a worrisome thought go.
    Notice what happens when a better thought pops into your head.
    When we listen to wisdom, caring and sharing happen naturally.

Chapter 4: Thinking too much can cover up your guide inside. Feelings let us know!
    You can be naturally aware of your feelings.
    It is easy to notice when feelings are changing.
    Learn to "Huli the bowl!" so helpful thoughts can create well-being.

Chapter 5: Knowing when to "Stop, Wait, Go" makes a big difference.
    Friends use their guide inside to make choices together.
    Friends acting from calm thinking show understanding and kindness.
    Friends know they can change their minds.

Chapter 6: Know who and what you are. You have well-being inside.
    Trust you do have personal well-being inside.
    You can accept support and make a healthy choice at any time!
    You will experience well-being by taking notice of your own insights.

Chapter 7: Learn to recognize your state of mind. Know it by the feeling you are in.
    When you focus attention, you will be aware of changes in your feelings.
    This means you are naturally listening to your guide inside.
    Helpful insights improve your feelings and natural motivation.

You are a Wonder

We have read a lot of stories in this book. We have been on a learning journey "*which expands our minds and lets us see beyond what we already know.*" (9)

It is fun to learn!

As we come to the end of this book, it is helpful to remember, "…one of the most fascinating and beautiful things in this life is realizing the powerful knowledge that lies within every person." (10)

This means you! This means me!

Here is simple advice for us. "Turn around, look within, and you will find the answer." (11)

Create a Belonging Map…
Note! Be thoughtful, show links; be accurate; make it easy to read.

Watch Video On Demand (VOD) to bring this chapter to life!
"Resources Tab" at myguideinside.com for VOD and Digital Media Options.
password: mgi

Stop and listen to your common sense…sometimes you seek help and sometimes you offer help. Create a "Belonging Map" with yourself in the center. Add names of people in your family, school, and community who can support you. Share your Belonging Map with an adult like a teacher or parent. Can the adult suggest other names you may choose to add?

Reflect and Write a Journal Entry…
Note! Use "I." Share your thoughts and feelings. Show insight and connections.

> ***"It is never too late to dream, and if your heart and thoughts
> are pure your dreams can come true." (12)***

Write about a dream you have for yourself. Discuss this dream with an adult like your teacher and/or parent.

Create a Personal Metaphor…
Note! Make your image strong, with true qualities, make good use of space, be neat.

Choose two words that describe you best.
Ask an adult to choose one word that describes you.
Create a picture, like an owl, and add the words below:

My guide inside is wise.
I am also_____, _____, and _____

Choose the three words from the many choices below:

balanced	fun-loving	patient
big-hearted	generous	polite
brave	grateful	practical
calm	happy	respectful
careful	helpful	responsible
caring	hopeful	relaxed
cheerful	humorous	secure
confident	imaginative	sensitive
co-operative	inventive	sharp
creative	kind	thankful
curious	light-hearted	trusting
easy-going	likable	thoughtful
energetic	lively	understanding
fair	loving	
friendly	open-minded	

 **Let's Revisit What You Know!**
Choose 2 or 3 of the ideas below that have meaning for you and discuss them.

- My guide inside is always there. 24-7-365.

- As soon as the cloudy thought passes by, "in its place comes a nicer thought that you act on." (4)

- Your guide inside is "powerful knowledge," also known as wisdom that
    - grows with you.
    - brings you love and compassion.
    - leads to the "joys of living."

- You have the gift of thought to use as you choose. Imagine that!

- You can drop a thought like a hot potato!

- Insights are helpful for knowing ourselves and understanding our world.

- Giving and receiving make a circle.

- Every child is born with a "Bowl of Light" filled with *aloha* and wisdom.

- RED light …STOP when angry!
  YELLOW light…What might this mean?
  GREEN light…GO ahead when at peace!

- Thought is a gift to use as you choose,
  Act on the good thoughts,
  And you'll have nothing to lose!

- To begin and keep healthy friendships, just be welcoming, friendly, and kind.

- Who and what you are inside is what counts.

- "Sometimes it was only their thoughts that were making them unhappy." (8)

- "Never forget one of the most fascinating and beautiful things in this life is realizing the powerful knowledge that lies within every person." (10)

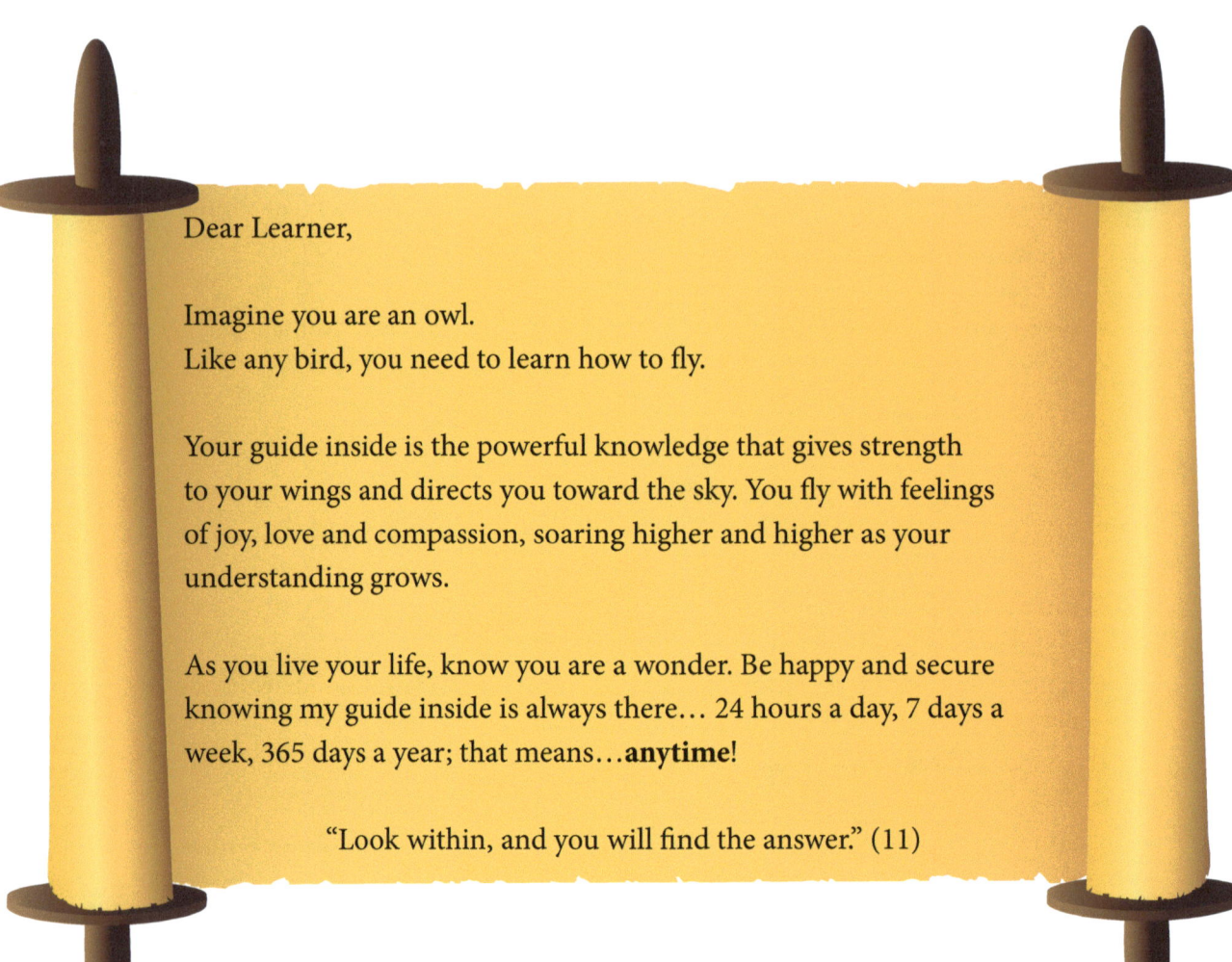

Dear Learner,

Imagine you are an owl.
Like any bird, you need to learn how to fly.

Your guide inside is the powerful knowledge that gives strength to your wings and directs you toward the sky. You fly with feelings of joy, love and compassion, soaring higher and higher as your understanding grows.

As you live your life, know you are a wonder. Be happy and secure knowing my guide inside is always there… 24 hours a day, 7 days a week, 365 days a year; that means…**anytime**!

"Look within, and you will find the answer." (11)

My Guide Inside® (Learner Book II)

Chapter 9
Power Words
Enriching Your
Life

Power Words Enriching Your Life

A
aloha—love (*Aloha* is a Hawaiian word)
aware—in the know, seeing what is

B
believe—accept as true
belonging—be a part of

C
calm—quiet
common sense—knowing to make good choices, insight, wisdom
compassion—caring
compassionately—with caring
confident—positive
confused—not clear
content—satisfied, happy
courage—power

D
decision—a choice

F
feeling—sense
fooled—tricked

G
grateful—feeling thanks
guide—help

H
healthy—good
huli—turn around, turn over (*Huli* is a Hawaiian word)

I
ignore—do nothing
imagination—create in your mind
insecure—unsure
insight—a helpful new idea, common sense, my guide inside, wisdom
insightful—wise
inner—within, inside yourself

J
joy—happiness

K
know-how—knowledge or skill
knowledge—intelligence, understanding

L
logical—makes common sense

M
my guide inside—common sense, insight, my wisdom

N
negative—not helpful or useful

O
overshadowed—covered up

P
patient—calm
positive—good, useful

R
realize—see, understand
respect—see as worthy, honor

S
secure—safe
serious—stern
signal—sign
source—where something begins or comes from
spiritual—inner

T
temper—state of mind (angry or calm)
thought—power to create an idea

U
understand—to know
upset—worried

V
vision—idea

W
welcoming—kind
wisdom—knowing what is true or right, common sense, insight, my guide inside
worry—upset

End Notes for My Guide Inside

A Special Story

Mr. Sydney Banks, whose insight about the wisdom within everyone is at the heart of *My Guide Inside*, wrote a special book for young people called *Dear Liza*, about "a poor yet happy orphan girl living in the slums of 19th century London. From treasured letters left to her by her mother, Liza learns a unique understanding about life. In her special way, her quiet wisdom touches the hearts and lives of everyone she meets." (13)

Dear Liza is a wonderful story, filled with beautiful feelings, and we highly recommend it to you!

This book is one of the sources, listed below, of our quotes from Mr. Banks that are found throughout *My Guide Inside*.

Sources for quotes in *My Guide Inside*

When a quote is used in this book, it is followed by the number of the source (in parentheses). For example, the quote at the end of the first paragraph on this page is followed by (13) which is listed below—"Ibid" means it is from the same book as the one before, so (13) is also from Dear Liza, listed as (12). "Speaker" means the quote is from a recorded talk given by Mr. Banks.

1. Banks, S., (2003) Speaker
2. Banks, S., (2004) *Dear Liza*, 67.
3. Ibid., 70.
4. Banks, S., (2003) Speaker
5. Banks, S., *Dear Liza*, 71.
6. Banks, S., (1998) *The Missing Link*, 47.
7. Banks, S., *Dear Liza*, 71.
8. Ibid., 46.
9. Ibid., 61.
10. Ibid., 69.
11. Banks, S. (2007) Speaker
12. Banks, S., *Dear Liza*, 68.
13. Ibid., Back cover

Overview of My Guide Inside® Comprehensive Curriculum
Contact: myguideinside.com

My Guide Inside is a three-part, comprehensive, Pre-K-12 story-based curriculum covering developmentally appropriate topics, in an ongoing process of learning that extends throughout the entire school career. As a teacher, you choose the level of *My Guide Inside* that is just right for your students in your particular school system: **Book I** (introduction, primary), **Book II** (continuation, intermediate), and **Book III** (advanced, secondary). This allows school leaders to chart a continuous instructional plan to share the Three Principles with students through the grades.

My Guide Inside, Book II offers Stories and Activities Designed for Success
Reading Level: "easy to read" (age 9-13)
Flexibility: regular course or adapt or modify to suit individual learners
Settings: classroom, small group or individual
Design: inclusive of self-directed learners working independently
Digital Media: Resources at myguideinside.com
Ideal Time: start of a program or school year to build community and foster optimism

Objectives of My Guide Inside (Book II): The principles discussed in this learner book operate in all people, including children. This curriculum introduces the way to wholeness, happiness, creativity and well-being in all parts of life. Therefore, *MGI* has these two globally appropriate academic goals, to:
(1) Enhance Personal Well-being with an understanding of these principles, and
(2) Develop competencies in Communication, Thinking, and Personal and Social Awareness and Responsibility.
MGI accomplishes both goals by using stories, discussion and various written and creative activities, as the learning increases your students' competency in English Language Arts and several other areas.

Discovering their guide inside is key to learning, and it enhances children's ability to make decisions, navigate life, and build healthy relationships. Accessing this natural wisdom affects well-being, spiritual wellness, personal and social responsibility, and positive personal and cultural identity. Social and emotional learning, including self-determination, self-regulation, and self-efficacy, is also a natural outcome of greater awareness of one's own inner wisdom/"guide inside." This understanding maximizes personal well-being and improves school climate, learner behavior, and academic performance. See what kids think: watch the *My Guide Inside* Overview (5min) and Focus Group Experiences with *My Guide Inside* video of secondary student outcomes: 5min summary or full 27min interview myguideinside.com.

Learning, Living, Sharing: The feeling a MGI teacher brings to the classroom every day, the "essential curriculum," is the greatest resource for directly impacting students. In other words, learning allows a teacher to live the principles by being in a natural state of service; sharing compassion, understanding and joy in the classroom. Once a teacher is being that informally and naturally, the teacher will be sharing the principles, via a positive feeling. This will enhance and make more powerful any formal lesson sharing with students. A teacher's own deep understanding and experience of these principles will bring out the best in all students. As each teacher continually learns and lives the principles, sharing this understanding with students becomes highly effective.

The Teacher's Manual for each book contains lesson plans, pre- and post-assessments, activities, evaluation scales, and online resources. Based on universal principles, this curriculum is designed for global use with all learners. Curriculum guidelines from Canada, the United Kingdom, and the United States guide this work.

Instructional Materials for Pre K — 12 Learners

My Guide Inside® Pre-K–12 Comprehensive Curriculum
Campsall, C. with Marshall Emerson, K. (2018). *My Guide Inside, Learner Book I.*
Campsall, C. with Marshall Emerson, K. (2018). *My Guide Inside, Teacher's Manual, Book I.*
Campsall, C., Tucker, J. (2016). *My Guide Inside, Learner Book II.*
Campsall, C. with Marshall Emerson, K. (2016). *My Guide Inside, Teacher's Manual, Book II.*
Campsall, C. with Marshall Emerson, K. (2017). *My Guide Inside, Learner Book III.*
Campsall, C. with Marshall Emerson, K. (2017). *My Guide Inside, Teacher's Manual, Book III.*

Picture Book (Pre-K)
Campsall, C., Tucker, J. (2018). *Whooo ... has a Guide Inside?*

Supplemental
Marshall Emerson, K. (2020). *Parenting with Heart.*
Tucker, J. (2020). *Insights: Messages of Hope, Peace and Love.*

My Guide Inside® is available through myguideinside.com
Check the website for:
E-books, MGI Online for schools, Video On Demand, Resources, Translations and More…

About the Authors

Christa Campsall has a 40+ year legacy teaching the principles shared in MGI. This has been the foundation of her work as a classroom teacher, learning services teacher in special education and school-based team chair. She has a BEd and DiplSpEd from University of British Columbia, and a MA from Royal Roads University. Along with MGI curriculum development, Christa facilitates professional development for educators in the global community. She and her husband live on Salt Spring Island, British Columbia.

Jane Tucker first heard Sydney Banks speak in 1976, and the knowledge he shared became the foundation for her many years working with children and youth as a "specials" teacher, tutor, and youth education outreach coordinator. She remained in close communication with Mr. Banks until his passing, and received certification from him to teach the Three Principles. Jane has a BA in English from Hood College and lives with her husband on Salt Spring Island, British Columbia.

What Teachers Say about *My Guide Inside*

"These authentic stories are simple, yet profound, and have the capacity to lead students to their guide inside."

Barb Aust, BEd, MEd, Principal, Education Consultant and Author, Salt Spring Island, BC, CA

"As a headteacher (principal) for over thirty years, I have often witnessed first-hand the restless struggles many children and youth experience as they begin to feel comfortable in their own skin. Christa, Kathy and Jane's straightforward, simple but profound curriculum helps teachers to point youth in a different direction, to our Guide Inside, our essence, our wisdom. I would recommend this guide to teachers as a powerful source of support. It helps us all remember who we really are ... pure love."

Peter Anderson, Cert. Edn. Adv. Diploma (Cambridge) Three Principles Facilitator, Headteacher Advisor, Essex, UK

"I have been a teacher in underserved schools in Baltimore, Miami and the Bronx for over 12 years. By sharing the simple understanding that students are able to decide how they wish to experience life through their choices about thought, I have seen aggressive students become peacemakers, shy, self-conscious children become confident leaders, and the level of consciousness and empathy raised in an entire school. I am thrilled that this curriculum will be seen and experienced by so many! This understanding has the power to change education and the school experience on a global scale!"

Christina G Puccio, BEd, MEd Teacher/Mentor Teacher, PS 536, Bronx, N.Y. US

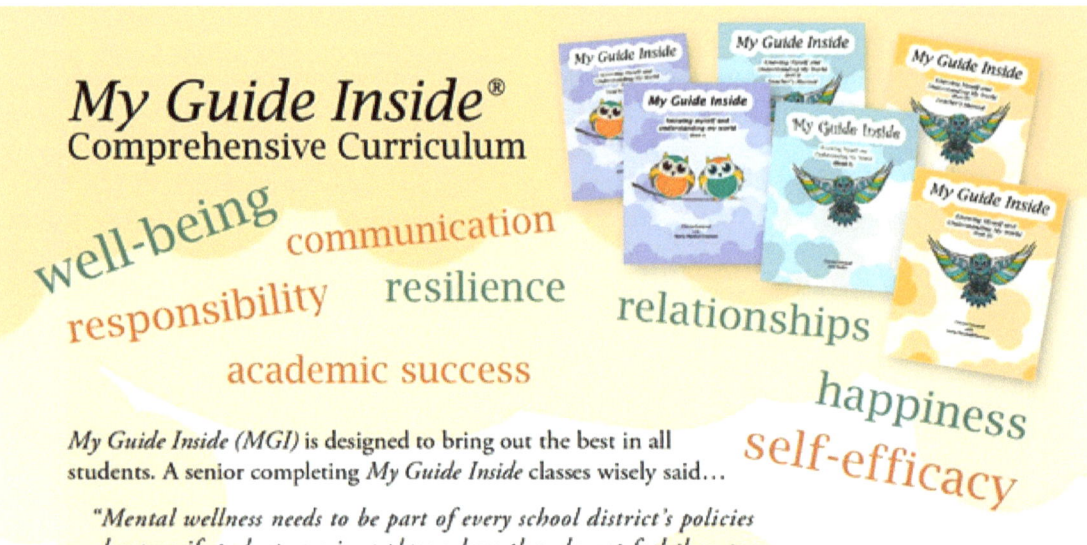

For other My Guide Inside offerings, see
myguideinside.com